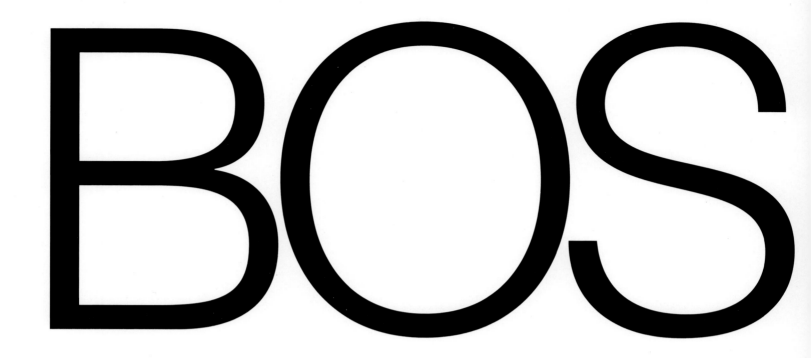

INTRODUCTION

HISTORY AND HERITAGE

THE HUB

CITY OF NEIGHBORHOODS

URBAN SANCTUARIES

A CITY TO LIVE IN

This edition published in 1992
by SMITHMARK Publishers Inc.,
112 Madison Avenue,
New York, New York 10016.

SMITHMARK books are available for bulk purchase
for sales promotion and premium use. For details
write or telephone the Manager of Special Sales,
SMITHMARK Publishers Inc., 112 Madison Avenue,
New York, NY 10016. (212) 532-6600.

Produced by Brompton Books Corp.,
15 Sherwood Place,
Greenwich, CT 06830.

ISBN 0-8317-0805-0

Printed in Hong Kong

10 9 8 7 6 5 4 3 2 1

Entrepreneurs also developed new industries, the largest of which was textile manufacturing.

As the economy improved, the population of the city increased from 6000 during the war with England to over 30,000 by 1810. During this period the building trades were active, constructing new markets, streets, churches, and public buildings, as well as luxurious mansions and town-houses designed by the well-known architect Charles Bulfinch.

Many of New England's thriving cotton textile factories were backed by the money of wealthy Boston families. Marriages between these new manufacturers and old Boston families led to the formation of an elite class of people known as Boston 'Brahmins,' a group which would greatly influence the city's development in the nineteenth century.

In the 1820s, under the leadership of Mayor Josiah Quincy, the city underwent a period of revitalization featuring essential public health measures such as garbage collection, street cleaning and a sewage system. Under Quincy's leadership the city developed fire and police departments and a welfare system.

Many people, however, were not satisfied with the limited scope of the reforms taking place. They believed that deeper social injustices were not being addressed, and during the 1830s and 1840s several more radical reform movements developed which emphasized the idea of equality. A women's movement challenged traditional British legal customs which considered women to be the property of their husbands and fathers and which prohibited them from voting, holding political office, or entering professions.

INTRODUCTION

Boston, the capital of Massachusetts and one of America's oldest cities, is a place of ever-changing people and ways. Founded by a group of people whose way of life conflicted with that of its leaders, Boston's very creation was rooted in a need for change.

Boston's first settlers left England to escape the rule of King James and his demand for full adherence to the practices of the Church of England. Religious pressures and economic depression forced large numbers of dissenters out of England during the late 1620s and early 1630s. Many ships sailed to America, and hundreds of people settled in the town of Boston. These settlers made a living by farming and by developing a thriving business of shipbuilding and of trade from Boston's large, well-protected harbor. In this way, Boston became virtually independent of England.

In the 1760s, the British government passed several restrictive laws, including taxes on various imported products. The American colonies resisted the new restrictions primarily by boycotting British goods. Britain was finally forced to repeal most taxes, but maintained the tax on tea. In the 'Boston Tea Party' of 1773, angry Bostonians led by Samuel Adams boarded British ships which carried tea, and dumped the cargo into the harbor.

The Revolutionary War officially began in 1775, and lasted for several years. Boston paid an enormous price in this brutal war. Many lives were lost, buildings were destroyed, and the city's economic structure was devastated. Soon after the war, merchants began to rebuild the economy and reestablished vigorous trade with the West Indies and South America.

ACKNOWLEDGMENTS

The author wishes to thank Adam Burrows, Lisa Kessler, and Sophie Burrows Ghitman for all of their help and inspiration. Thanks also to Rita Longabucco, the photo editor; and Jean Chiaramonte Martin, the editor.

1 An inviting doorway to a townhouse in the elegant district of Beacon Hill.

3-6 This panoramic view shows off Boston's gleaming harbor, as well as an impressive skyline with the Charles River in the background.

8

TON

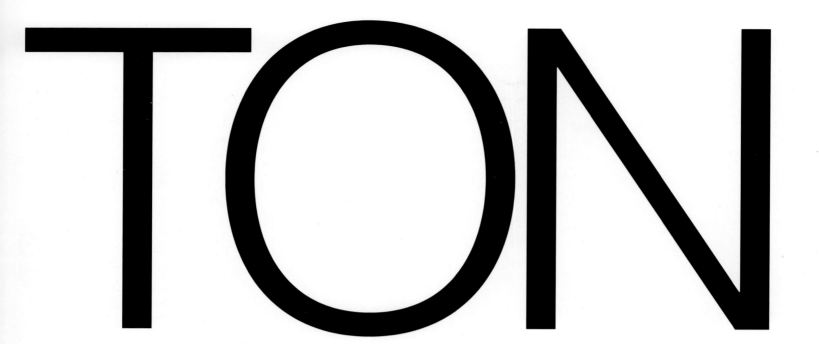

TEXT   JANE-MARIE GHITMAN

DESIGN   DON LONGABUCCO

SMITHMARK

Another logical consequence of the emphasis on equality was the antislavery movement, which was growing throughout the country. The newspaper *The Liberator*, published in Boston by William Lloyd Garrison, incited Southern slaves to revolt. This movement blossomed quickly in Boston, and eventually the abolitionist movement focused on discrimination in Boston itself. Until this time, Boston's blacks had been limited to menial jobs, segregated into separate train cars, and excluded from many public places. Blacks were barred from the public school system until 1854, when the legislature finally prohibited the exclusion of any child from school based on race, color or religion.

From the late 1820s to the 1850s, Boston received a large, sudden influx of Catholic immigrants, primarily from Ireland. The newcomers arrived in enormous numbers: while the previous immigration rate had been four to five thousand a year, in 1847 alone over 37,000 Irish arrived in Boston. Bringing a different religion and a different way of life, the Irish were greatly feared and mistrusted by the established residents.

The Civil War provided Bostonians with a common cause, and relations between these two groups improved somewhat during and after the war. In the late nineteenth century the social standing of the Irish began to improve. Modernization of the city during this time, including the expansion of many services to the city's inhabitants, provided jobs for immigrants. Meanwhile, the Irish entered the political arena, and in 1884 Hugh O'Brien was elected the first Irish mayor.

Throughout the nineteenth century, immigrants from all parts of the world continued to arrive, including Italians, Jews, Poles, Russians, and Greeks. Many of the city's wealthier citizens responded by leaving the city for surrounding towns and suburbs.

During the early twentieth century, children of the original Irish immigrants played an important role in the development of a Democratic party to rival the Brahmin Republicans. In 1913, Boston elected as mayor a young Irishman named James Michael Curley. During his three terms in office, Curley instituted many reforms, most of which helped the city's poor. Curley himself rose from poverty to considerable wealth, and served as a role model for the city's Irish poor.

From the 1940s to the early 1960s, under the leadership of mayors John Hynes and John Collins, the city embarked on many urban renewal projects. Federal dollars helped to support the construction of the Prudential Center, the revitalization of Copley Square, the downtown shopping area, and the Quincy Market area, and the development of Government Center, the new City Hall, and the wharf area featuring the New England Aquarium. Computer and electronics industries sprouted up along Route 128, a beltway which encircles the city. These industries drew many professionals out of the city, and once again the population of the city declined.

During the 1960s and 1970s, as the African-American population grew, so did its pride in its heritage and discontent with social and economic inequities. Around the country, as in Boston, African-Americans demanded equal rights in housing, education and employment. Students in all parts of the country demonstrated against racial inequities. As a city of colleges and universities, Boston became a center for these struggles.

Throughout this troubled period, Mayor Kevin White managed to maintain the renewal projects begun by his predecessors. White worked to create a reputation for the city as a commercial, educational, and cultural metropolis with an important historical heritage. During this time, tourism increased, and the city attracted many scientists and scholars, young families, and new businesses. As jobs and cultural institutions grew, many young professionals moved back to the city from the suburbs.

The 1983 mayoral election was won by Raymond Flynn, an Irish Catholic from South Boston. During the early 1980s, the economy of the city, like that of the country as a whole, improved. With inflation down, industry increased and development continued. Large groups of immigrants continued to arrive from Southeast Asia, Latin America, the Caribbean, and other parts of the world. Mayor Flynn entered his third term with great popularity, facing the challenges of serving a truly multicultural population.

Over the course of its history, Boston has adapted to one crisis after another, and each period of adaptation has contributed to the texture of the city today. Boston's unique wealth of cultural resources, educational institutions, and progressive traditions continues to make it an attractive city to visit and to live in.

HISTORY AND HERITAGE

Colonial and revolutionary times are hundreds of years in our past, and can feel quite remote from today's modern life. But a journey along Boston's Freedom Trail, and a little imagination, can easily carry anyone back in time.

At the corner of the Boston Common is the Park Street Church, in which William Lloyd Garrison gave his first antislavery speech in 1829. Behind the church lies the Old Granary Burying Ground, where many of Boston's important historical figures are buried. The Massachusetts State House, on Beacon Street, is a masterpiece of neoclassical architecture with its elegant Corinthian columns and an impressive gold-leafed dome.

In the blocks between Tremont and Washington streets are the site of the country's first public school; the Old Corner Bookstore, where Anne Hutchinson's home once stood; and King's Chapel, Boston's first Anglican church. The Old State House, on Washington Street, served a variety of important government functions throughout the eighteenth and nineteenth centuries. Benjamin Franklin's birthplace is a little farther down the street, along with the Old South Meeting House. This church has functioned more as a political than a religious institution; here the organizers of the Boston Tea Party met to plan their rebellion. Around the corner is the site of the Boston Massacre, in which British troops fired into a crowd of Bostonians, killing five people. A little farther on is Faneuil Hall, which was designed to house town meetings and a public marketplace. Some 250 years later, the building still serves both of its original functions.

In the North End is Paul Revere's home, the oldest house in Boston. Christ Church, known as 'Old North,' is just down the street. In 1775, Paul Revere hung his two lanterns from the steeple of this well-known church to signal the departure route of British soldiers. At the top of Copp's Hill is the Burying Ground where British troops fired practice shots, the marks of which can still be seen on some of the gravestones.

Across the Charles River, in Charlestown, is the USS *Constitution*, the oldest commissioned ship in the US Navy, and the Bunker Hill Monument, which commemorates the important battle which took place there in 1775. From this historic vantage point, a look back across the harbor reveals the gleaming skyline of a thriving modern city mingled with evidence of Boston's rich heritage as the 'Birthplace of Freedom.'

15 Old and new blend dramatically in Boston's Copley Square. Trinity Church was designed by H H Richardson and was completed in 1877. More than 100 years later, the John Hancock Tower, designed by I M Pei, added its mirrored face to this square. This tower is the tallest building in New England.

16-17 A warm summer day brings pushcarts and strollers to the busy marketplace at Faneuil Hall.

18 Faneuil Hall was originally constructed in 1742, and was reconstructed and enlarged by Charles Bulfinch in 1805. The building still serves as a meeting place for citizens' groups.

19 Quincy Market is busy day and night with people shopping and making merry in a variety of stores, restaurants and nightclubs. Also visible in this photograph is the beautifully illuminated clock of the Custom House Tower.

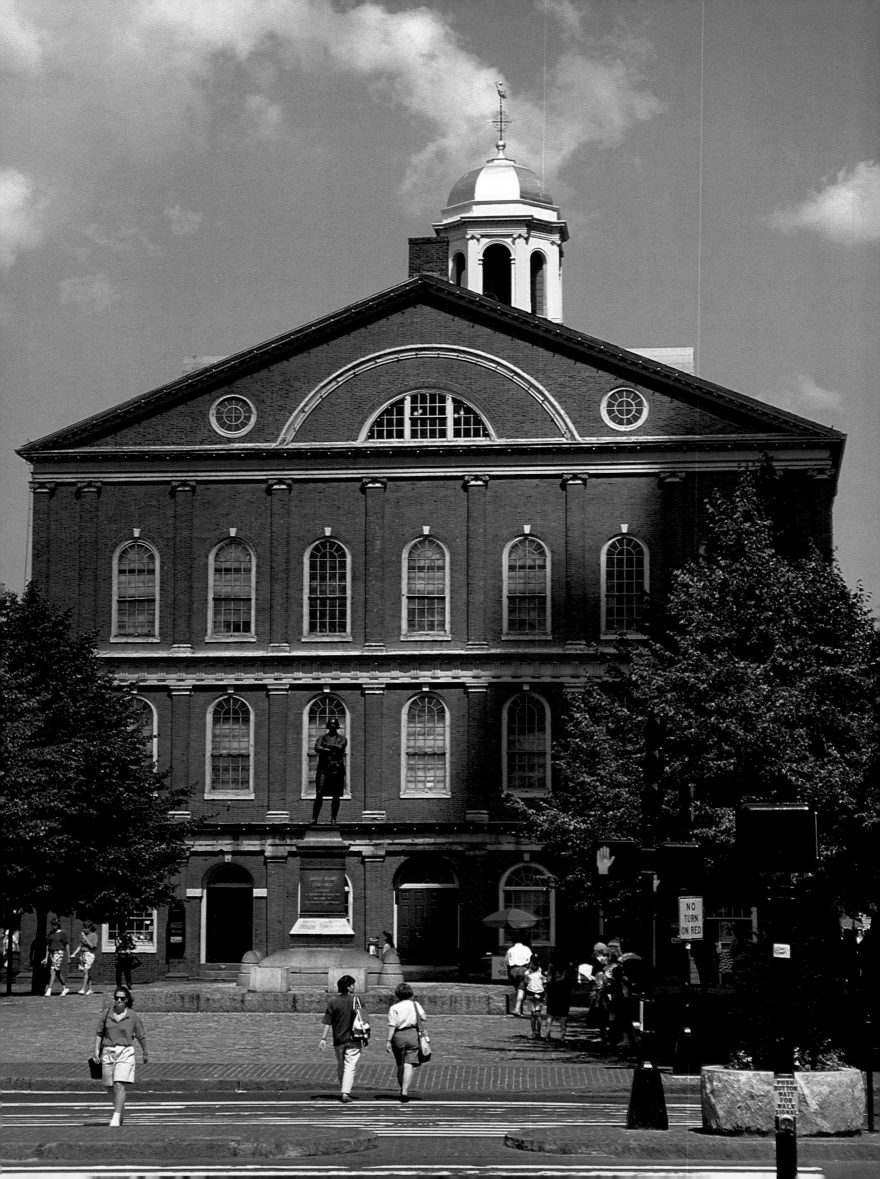

20 *The Old State House was built in 1713, and today houses a museum with a rich assortment of exhibits of historic interest.*

21 *This golden eagle, a detail from the Old State House, remains as a symbol of British power.*

22-23 *Union Oyster House, one of Boston's oldest restaurants, has been serving fresh seafood to 'ladies and gents' since 1826. The building itself dates from 1714.*

THE UNION BAR

LADIES & GEN

ye olde
UNION
OYSTER
HOUSE
est. 1826

UNION ST
MARSHALL ST

ye olde UNION OYSTER HOUSE est. 1826
The ORIGINAL OYSTER HOUSE

ye olde UNION OYSTER HOUSE est. 1826

S & GENTS   SEA GRILL

24 This bronze monument was sculpted by
Augustus Saint-Gaudens as a memorial to
Colonel Robert Gould Shaw, who died leading
a unit of free blacks in a Civil War battle in
South Carolina.

25 Old South Meeting House, a church built in
1729, has been the site of many historically
important events, including the meeting in
which the Boston Tea Party was planned.

26 Paul Revere's house, originally built in the 1680s, has been restored in recent years; but most of the framework and furniture is original. The table pictured here is set with pyramids of fruit for a 'First Night' celebration.

27 Old Granary Burying Ground is one of several historic cemeteries in Boston. Pictured here is the grave of Samuel Adams; others buried here include John Hancock, Paul Revere, Benjamin Franklin's parents and the five victims of the Boston Massacre.

28 The USS Constitution, *known as 'Old Ironsides' for its tough wooden hull. This 1797 ship is now docked in the Charlestown Navy Yard.*

29 The Beaver II *is a reproduction of one of the original Boston Tea Party ships. Visitors to this museum reenact this event by throwing symbolic cases of tea into the harbor.*

30-31 *On June 17th of every year, the Battle of Bunker Hill is reenacted on its original site. Ambitious visitors can climb the 294 steps to the top of the Bunker Hill Monument.*

32-33 *These beautifully decorated doors are typical of many in historic Beacon Hill.*

34 The quaint cobblestoned streets of Beacon
Hill have changed little in appearance since
their construction in the early nineteenth
century.

35 Warmly lit homes and streets illuminated by
gas lamps retain the original flavor of this
historic neighborhood.

36-37 The Massachusetts State House was
designed by Charles Bulfinch and completed
in 1798.

38 The Hall of Flags is one of many decorated rooms inside the State House.

39 Christ Church, known as 'Old North,' is the oldest church in Boston. An active Episcopal congregation still enjoys the simple beauty of this church's interior.

40-41 The elegant University Museum building houses four of the seven museums administered by Harvard University. The building exhibits zoological, archaeological, botanical, and mineral collections.

THE HUB

Every city offers its particular diversions and pleasures to residents and visitors. Boston has an unusually rich assortment of educational institutions, performance spaces, museums, and other sources of entertainment.

An emphasis on education developed early in Boston's history. Harvard College was founded in 1636, and in 1642 laws were passed requiring parents to educate their children. These laws led to the creation of the country's first public school system in 1647. Today the Boston area is home to over 150 colleges and universities and several important research institutions.

Student life characterizes the atmosphere of parts of the Boston area. Bookstores, cafes, and a lively nightlife abound in Harvard Square, while aspiring musicians fill the streets near the Berkelee School of Music and the New England Conservatory.

Boston also has a rich selection of museums. In addition to the world-renowned Museum of Fine Arts, there are dozens of smaller art museums. Boston is also home to several unique theme museums, including the Children's Museum, the Museum of Science, the New England Sports Museum, and the Computer Museum.

Boston is a center for music, and boasts several highly regarded music schools, a world class symphony orchestra, and many smaller ensembles. Boston hosts several annual music festivals, and summer concerts by the Boston Pops and other groups on the Charles River. Many young musicians come to Boston to pursue music studies, and its nightclubs are filled with budding talents. A number of well-known jazz and popular musicians launched their careers in this city.

In the worlds of music and art, Boston supports not only well-known, mainstream talents, but also a substantial number of independent artists. Comedy clubs also abound, and have over the years presented several now-famous comedians.

Last but certainly not least is Boston's devotion to sports. Fenway Park, home of baseball's Boston Red Sox, rises proudly from the heart of the city. The basketball Celtics and the hockey Bruins have raised many championship banners at the Boston Garden. Pennant races and playoff competitions rally the city to annual frenzies of civic unity.

43 A statue of John Harvard watches over the pristine campus of the university to which he donated a large book collection and gave his name.

44-45 The Massachusetts Institute of Technology, known worldwide for its contributions to the sciences, sits proudly on the banks of the Charles River in Cambridge. The MIT campus includes a wide variety of architectural styles; pictured here is an august example of its neoclassical buildings.

46 The headquarters of the Harvard Medical School is a grand, impressive building. The world-renowned educational and research establishment is affiliated with several prestigious local hospitals.

47 Boston University, one of over 150 colleges and universities serving the Boston area, enrolls close to 20,000 students in its undergraduate and graduate programs. Shown here is the part of the campus known as 'BU Beach,' where students study and sunbathe near the banks of the Charles River.

48 The Museum of Fine Arts ranks among the world's most respected art museums. Exhibits include extensive collections of American, Asiatic, and European art, textiles, costumes, and early musical instruments.

49 This magnificent courtyard is at the center of the Italian-style mansion built by Isabella Stewart Gardner around the turn of the century to hold her eclectic art collection. This impressive collection includes paintings, sculpture, furniture and textiles. The museum also hosts concerts several times a week.

50-51 A brightly colored kinetic sculpture of a lobster greets visitors to the New England Aquarium, located along the Boston Harbor waterfront. The Aquarium boasts the world's largest salt water tank.

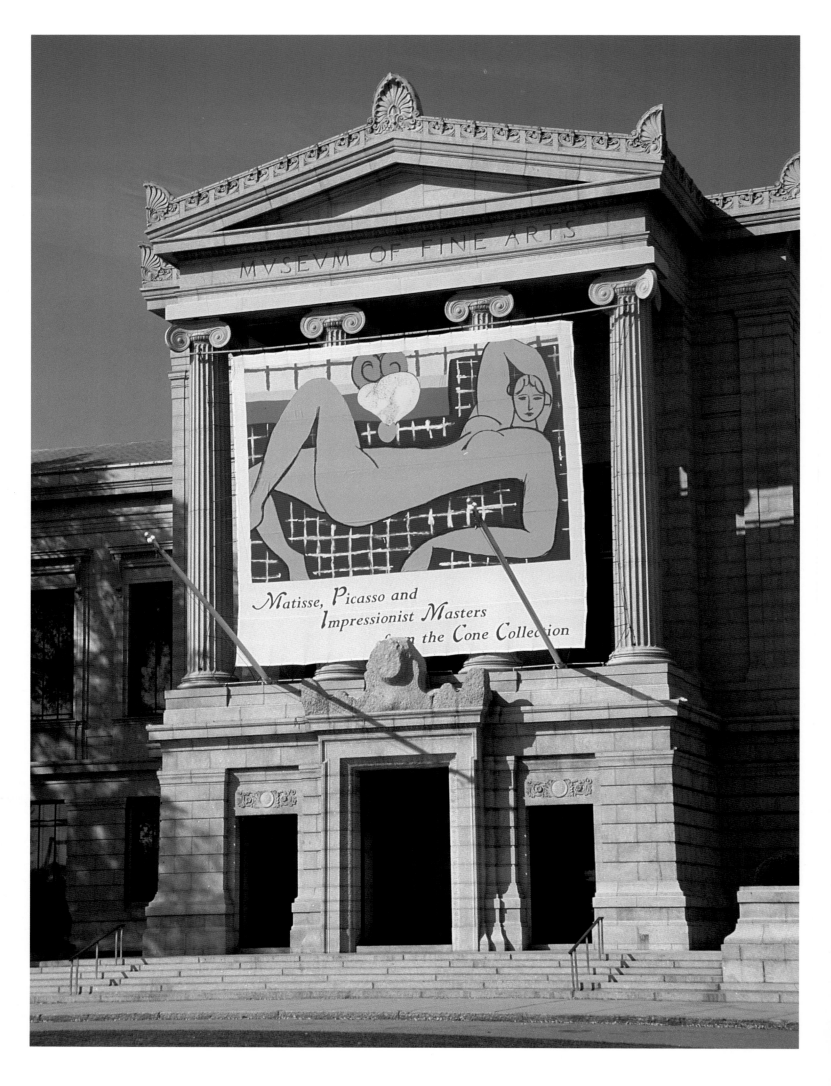

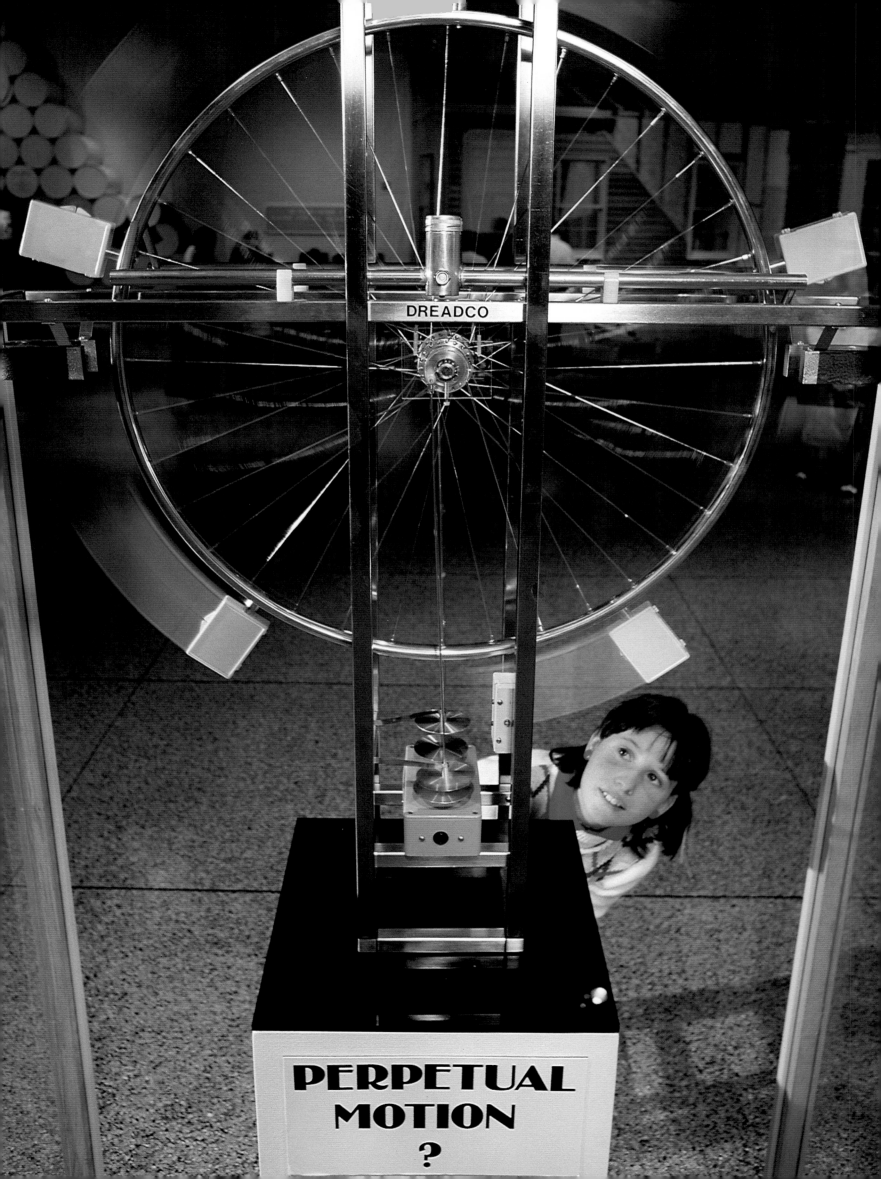

DREADCO

PERPETUAL
MOTION
?

52 A youngster learns through play with one of
the many interactive exhibits found in the
Museum of Science.

53 An audience enjoys a classical concert on
a pleasant summer evening at the Hatchshell.

54 The Boston Marathon is perhaps the city's most popular annual event. Every Patriot's Day, thousands gather on rooftops and sidewalks to cheer the runners on.

55 Devoted fans of the Boston Celtics basketball team fill the Boston Garden, which is also home to the city's hockey team, the Bruins.

56-57 Fenway Park, a green haven in the heart of the city, is one of the country's oldest and most intimate baseball parks. Here fans gather to hope for a Red Sox home run over the infamous 'Green Monster.'

58-59 Harvard University's football stadium draws alumni, students and other fans for the oldest rivalry in Ivy League sports, the annual Harvard-Yale game.

60 The handsome Boston Public Library is a priceless resource for the city. The library houses numerous literary, government, and media collections. In the background of this photo is the Prudential Tower.

61 The interior of the Boston Public Library is decorated with sculptures and murals by well-known artists such as Louis Saint-Gaudens, Edwin Austin Abbey, and John Singer Sargent.

62-63 This striking profile of the John Fitzgerald Kennedy Library shows off its architectural boldness. The building, designed by I M Pei, serves as both a resource for research and as a museum, with exhibits highlighting Kennedy's life and career.

CITY OF NEIGHBORHOODS

Bostonians are proud of their neighborhoods, and the curious visitor will discover the charms of urban community life. The city's self-contained neighborhoods provide residents with a sense of identity and of continuity.

A visitor to Boston today can wander through the North End tasting Italian delicacies and, if the timing is right, be swept up in the celebration of a traditional Italian festival. In the Hyde Square area of Jamaica Plain, Salsa music fills the air, and just down the road one can choose from several corner pubs which offer Irish food and music. In neighborhoods such as the Back Bay and Beacon Hill along the banks of the Charles River, one can stroll through cobble-stoned streets lit by gas lamps.

Boston today is an amalgam of ethnic neighborhoods. Although the geographic location of these ethnic enclaves has changed over time, the inhabitants of these neighborhoods have contributed to the city's personality from early in its history. While Boston's population came primarily from England during the seventeenth and eighteenth centuries, groups of Irish, Italians, Greeks, Germans, Jews, Poles and Russians began to arrive in the early nineteenth century. Later, large numbers of immigrants gravitated to Boston from various parts of Latin America, the Caribbean, and Asia.

Throughout Boston's history, the structure of many of its neighborhoods has been strongly influenced by the Catholic Church. While this structure has changed along with shifting demographics, many neighborhoods were long ago divided into parishes, and today people often still use their parish names instead of street addresses.

From its earliest days to the present, Boston has continually adapted in response to the needs of its changing inhabitants, who have arrived from all parts of the world. Change has not always been smooth, as the needs of diverse groups of people have often come into conflict. But cities are defined by the people who inhabit them, and Boston is a fine example of the human tapestry characteristic of great American cities.

65 Union Park in the South End is a fine example of efforts to restore the original beauty of the neighborhood's classic brownstones and gardens.

66-67 A wall mural on Newbury Street depicts a woman window-shopping, a common sight on one of the city's most fashionable shopping strips.

68 On a pleasant stroll down Newbury Street, the visitor might be lured into bookstores, cafes, art galleries or clothing boutiques.

69 When the weather permits, Boston's sidewalk cafes come to life. Pictured here is a cafe on Newbury Street.

70-71 Restaurants abound in the historic North End, a neighborhood now inhabited primarily by Italians. Pictured here is North Square, a site featured along the Freedom Trail.

72 Harvard Square always buzzes with
students and visitors who come to enjoy its
street performers, eateries, and bohemian
atmosphere.

73 Horatio Harris Park, in the residential
neighborhood of Roxbury, was created in
honor of an antique dealer who once lived on
this square.

74 Chinatown in Boston is a busy neighborhood of ethnic restaurants and numerous small businesses.

75 Each year Vietnamese Catholic girls in native dress celebrate World Mission Day with dozens of other ethnic Catholic groups at the Cathedral of the Holy Cross, in the South End.

76-77 St Patrick's Day in Boston is celebrated with great enthusiasm and pride by the city's many Irish inhabitants. Here, two generations march together, displaying the flag of Ireland.

78-79 A colorful mural decorates a wall at Villa Victoria, a housing development in the South End inhabited by many Latin American immigrants. Villa Victoria's Jorge Hernandez Cultural Center brings many world-renowned musicians to Boston.

80 For children living in the city, the streets provide many opportunities for creative play.

81 A number of fountains around the city provide relief from the summer heat. Here, a boy cools off in the fountain at the Christian Science Church.

82 South Boston residents relax during a visit to one of their neighborhood's loveliest spots, Castle Island.

83 Young Bostonians keep up with current fashion trends, as demonstrated by this young man's hair style and jacket.

URBAN SANCTUARIES

Natural beauty abounds in the city of Boston. Its location between the Atlantic coast and the beautiful Charles River has contributed greatly to its appeal. As the city has grown over the past two centuries, city planners have fortunately had the foresight to preserve large tracts from development.

Many of the larger parks were designed toward the end of the nineteenth century. The 'Emerald Necklace' is a chain of parks designed by the well-known landscape architect Frederick Law Olmsted. The jewels of the necklace include Franklin Park, with its zoo, golf course, and riding stables; the Back Bay Fens, featuring an unusual assortment of landscapes built on marshland; Jamaica Pond, which offers fishing, sailing and rowing; and the Arnold Arboretum, which serves as a botanical laboratory and is home to over 14,000 varieties of plants. Further from the center of the city is the Blue Hills Reservation, which offers ski and hiking trails.

Every colonial New England town was built around a central common, and Boston is no exception. Cattle once grazed on the Boston Common, but today one is more likely to see people playing frisbee, flying kites, or having a picnic. The adjacent Public Garden is the oldest botanical garden in the United States.

The seacoast provides another rich source of outdoor activities. Boat rides are available to many of the islands in Boston's harbor, or to watch whales during their yearly migration. There are beaches right in the city, in the neighborhoods of Dorchester and South Boston, as well as many larger beaches within short driving distances and on several of the harbor islands. Sailing is also a popular activity, on the ocean, the Charles River, and the area's lakes and ponds.

85 A toddler watches a swan boat glide past in the Public Garden.

86-87 This bird's-eye view of downtown Boston shows the Boston Common in the foreground, the golden dome of the capitol building, the Park Street Church (at the far right corner of the Common), and the Boston Harbor in the background.

88 top Swan boats take a rest while waiting for passengers in the Public Garden.

88 bottom Brass ducks cross the grounds of the Public Garden on a snow-dusted winter day.

89 Children feed the feathered residents of the Public Garden, where pigeons share their urban home with swans and ducks.

90-91 Members of the Harvard rowing team work hard, but surely they appreciate the serene beauty of the Charles River.

92-93 A glimmering Boston skyline including the Prudential Tower and the old and new John Hancock buildings, separates a tranquil Charles River from an animated sky.

94 Memorial Drive is closed to traffic on
Sundays in summer, allowing for various forms
of recreation. Here, young rollerbladers
practice their slalom technique using plastic
cups as cones.

95 The Boston Common is beautiful in all
seasons; here, a light snow creates a peaceful
atmosphere for a winter walk. The steeple of
the Park Street Church is visible through the
branches.

96 The Kelleher Rose Garden is one of many
attractions in the beautifully landscaped Back
Bay Fens.

97 Every season shows off its best qualities in the Arnold Arboretum, in Jamaica Plain. Here picnickers and strollers enjoy the brilliant blooms of springtime.

98-99 A bicycle path runs parallel to the 'Orange Line' subway in the Southwest Corridor Park, offering commuters a choice of ways to travel to downtown Boston. The park and subway were built here instead of a planned major highway.

100 The Charles River Esplanade shows off its colors on a sunny autumn day.

101 A mother and child observe gorillas in the Tropical Rain Forest display at the recently renovated Franklin Park Zoo.

102-103 Jamaica Pond is one of the city's most popular parks in which to boat, fish, walk, jog, or just sit and relax. The boathouse, seen here, serves snacks year-round, and in winter visitors are warmed by its fireplace. Weekly evening concerts at the pavilion are free to the public.

A CITY TO LIVE IN

Above all else, Boston is a place in which people live. In this city, as in any American town, people gather for barbeques, play Little League baseball, gossip on front porches, and stroll in the park on Sundays. Through these and other activities Bostonians share a way of life with their fellow Americans around the country.

At the same time, Boston differs from small-town America in significant ways. Most importantly, Boston is a modern city which is constantly working to keep up with the needs of its inhabitants. A good example of this is the city's extensive transportation system. Commuters from surrounding suburbs can travel to downtown Boston by bus, train, or boat. Within the city, a fascinating network of trolleys, subways, above-ground trains and buses carry people to and from every neighborhood and even to distant suburbs. Many stations of the Massachusetts Bay Transit Authority are decorated with local artwork and poetry.

Elsewhere in the city, signs of modernity abound. The wharf area has been revitalized in recent years with new commercial and residential spaces such as Quincy Market and the glamorous Rowe's Wharf. Local citizens and tourists also enjoy new waterfront promenades, cafes, and a variety of harbor cruises.

Thanks to its geographic location, Bostonians can sail their boats in the harbor or enjoy fresh lobster in waterfront restaurants. This seaside location also supports important sectors of the economy, including fishing, lobstering, and the restaurant industry.

Boston has suffered many of the difficulties which confront all American cities, and has shared in the nation's economic and political struggles. But Boston, as always, responds with vitality to its challenges. Its dynamic past and present demonstrate that it will thrive, while continually changing, for many years to come.

105 A 'Red Line' train streaks across the Longfellow Bridge, surrounded by the lights of the Boston skyline and a marina on the Charles River. The Prudential Tower is visible in the background.

106-107 A full moon adds light to a brilliant skyline, showing the old and new John Hancock buildings and the Charles River.

108 The pedestrian mall at Downtown
Crossing always bustles with pushcart
vendors, shoppers, and local workers on
lunch break.

109 A summer evening concert draws a
colorful crowd to City Hall Plaza.

110 A view of the Boston Harbor from a downtown skyscraper shows the Custom House Tower in the foreground, the New England Aquarium behind it, and the Southeast Expressway running along the waterfront.

*111 This view of the waterfront seen from the
Boston Harbor shows off Rowe's Wharf, an
elegant complex of apartments, offices,
restaurants and shops.*

112 Sumptuous fruit and a young vendor beckon to shoppers at Haymarket, Boston's largest outdoor produce and fish market.

113 Haymarket offers the best prices in town for fish fresh from the ocean.

114-115 A mighty little tugboat helps a massive freighter enter the harbor to unload its cargo.

116 Lobsters abound in the cold waters surrounding Boston. In 1990 alone, over one million lobsters were caught by Boston lobstermen.

117 Construction workers raise a heavy load at a building site in Boston.

118-119 Gleaming fire engines prepare for their call to action at a station on Boylston Street.

120 'Cheers,' the bar made famous by a television series, remains a popular place for tourists and locals to gather for a drink.

121 This inviting restaurant in Boston's Back Bay is one of many fine seafood establishments which serve the bounty of local waters.

122 The Mother Church of Christian Scientists, originally established in Boston in 1882, has since become an enormous complex including the offices of the Christian Science Monitor, administrative buildings, and a 670-foot reflecting pool.

123 The Greater Boston area is a center for the development of many new technologies. Here, a speech scientist investigates potential uses of artificial intelligence.

124 The Airport Water Shuttle, which carries
passengers from Rowe's Wharf to Logan
Airport, is an appealing alternative to the
traffic-congested highway. Other boat shuttles
carry commuters from Boston to surrounding
towns and to the Harbor Islands.

125 The morning rush hour can be hectic at the South Station train depot, located in the heart of the city. The recently renovated building contains restaurants, bookstores and a variety of other services useful to commuters arriving on business and to tourists.

126-127 A graceful footbridge crosses the lagoon at the Public Garden.

128 The warm evening sun silhouettes downtown buildings, as a family goes for a leisurely sail in the Boston Harbor.